TRUCKS

PICKUPS TO BIG RIGS

Adrianna Morganelli

x1000r/min

CRABTREE PUBLISHING COMPANY
www.crabtreebooks.com

Crabtree Publishing Company
www.crabtreebooks.com

For Allison, Carrie, Ellen, Michelle, Rachel, Rosie, and Samara
To a new beginning ...

Coordinating editor: Ellen Rodger
Series editor: Rachel Eagen
Project Editor: L. Michelle Nielsen
Editor: Carrie Gleason
Design and production coordinator: Rosie Gowsell
Cover design, layout, and production assistance: Samara Parent
Art direction: Rob MacGregor
Photo research: Allison Napier
Prepress technician: Nancy Johnson

Photo Credits: David Hoffman Photo Library/Alamy: p. 24 (top); LOOK Die Bildagentur der Fotografen GmbH/Alamy: p. 17 (top); Willy Matheisl/Alamy: p. 16 (bottom); Bob Pardue/Alamy: p. 19 (top); Performance Image/Alamy: 4 (top); POPPERFOTO/Alamy: p. 9 (bottom); The Print Collector/Alamy: p. 7 (bottom); Linda Richards/Alamy: p. 26; Jack Sullivan/Alamy: p. 21 (bottom); Thinkstock / Alamy: p. 7 (top); Transtock Inc./Alamy: p. 30 (bottom); Martyn Vickery/Alamy: p. 15 (top); Visions of America, LLC/Alamy: p. 17 (bottom); AP Photo/The Grand Island Independent, Barrett Stinson: p. 28; AP Photo/David Zalubowski: p. 27 (bottom); AP Photo/ U.S. Air Force /Tech. Sgt Joe Zuccaro, HO: p. 31; David Allio/Icon SMI/Corbis: p. 27 (top); Rob Howard/Corbis: p. 12; Dick Reed/Corbis: p. 1; Roger Ressmeyer/Corbis: p. 5 (bottom); Ian Schein Photography/Corbis: p. 24 (bottom); The Granger Collection, New York: p. 6; Mary Evans Picture Library/The Image Works: p. 9 (top); NRM/SSPL/The Image Works: p. 8; Jim West/The Image Works: p. 4 (bottom), p. 18; Katherine Kantor: cover, pp. 10-11, p. 16 (top), p. 29; Ron Kimball/Ron Kimball Stock: p. 20 (top), p. 30 (top); David Grossman/Photo Researchers, Inc.: p. 5.

Special thanks to
Bill Baker and Dean Auger of W.A. Baker Trucking

Cover: Monster trucks show what they can do, such as crushing cars and jumping over obstacles, in large arenas or stadiums. Thousands of screaming fans come to watch.

Title page: This Hummer is a sports utility vehicle, or SUV. Its design is based on the Humvee, a vehicle made for military use.

Library and Archives Canada Cataloguing in Publication

Morganelli, Adrianna, 1979-
    Trucks : pickups to big rigs/ Adrianna Morganelli.

(Automania!)
Includes index.
ISBN 978-0-7787-3015-6 (bound)
ISBN 978-0-7787-3037-8 (pbk.)

    1. Trucks--Juvenile literature. I. Title. II. Series.

TL230.15.M67 2007   j629.224   C2007-900647-7

Library of Congress Cataloging-in-Publication Data

Morganelli, Adrianna, 1979-
    Trucks : pickups to big rigs / written by Adrianna Morganelli.
      p. cm. -- (Automania!)
    Includes index.
    ISBN-13: 978-0-7787-3015-6 (rlb)
    ISBN-10: 0-7787-3015-8 (rlb)
    ISBN-13: 978-0-7787-3037-8 (pb)
    ISBN-10: 0-7787-3037-9 (pb)
    1. Trucks--Juvenile literature. I. Title. II. Series.

TL230.15.M675 2007
629.224--dc22

2007003402

Crabtree Publishing Company
www.crabtreebooks.com   1-800-387-7650

Published in Canada
Crabtree Publishing
616 Welland Ave.
St. Catharines, ON
L2M 5V6

Published in the United States
Crabtree Publishing
PMB16A
350 Fifth Ave., Suite 3308
New York, NY 10118

Published in the United Kingdom
Crabtree Publishing
White Cross Mills
High Town, Lancaster
LA1 4XS

Published in Australia
Crabtree Publishing
386 Mt. Alexander Rd.
Ascot Vale (Melbourne)
VIC 3032

Contents

Keep on Truckin'

Trucks are powerful motor vehicles designed to transport cargo, or goods. They have many of the same basic parts as regular passenger cars, but are built with special features that allow them to haul heavy loads and travel on rough terrain. Trucks serve other functions as well, such as providing emergency services.

Straight and Articulated

There are two main types of trucks – straight and articulated. Straight trucks are made using one chassis. A chassis is the frame that supports the truck's engine, cabin, and bed, or area where cargo is stored. Straight trucks include pickup trucks, sport utility vehicles, or SUVs, garbage trucks, and delivery trucks. Articulated trucks, also called tractor-trailers, are made up of two separate parts that are connected by **couplings**. The front section is called the tractor, and contains the engine and the cabin, or the enclosed area where the driver and passengers sit. The back section is the trailer, which has its own set of wheels. Articulated trucks are often about 80 feet (24 meters) long, and their powerful engines allow them to haul heavy cargo.

(above) This 1950s pickup has been restored using features, such as whitewall tires, that were popular when the model was first made.

(left) SUVs are popular because they are large and stylish. This SUV is a hybrid, which means it runs on gasoline and electricity, making it more environmentally-friendly.

Designed to Haul

Different kinds of trucks are designed to do specific jobs. Ambulances and fire trucks are used to assist in emergency situations. They are equipped with powerful engines to reach emergency sites quickly, and carry special equipment for emergency care. Many different **industries** use trucks. The construction industry uses many types of trucks, such as dump trucks, which are used to transport gravel, dirt, sand, and materials to and away from job sites. The logging industry provides wood to customers using flatbed trucks to deliver the logs. Trucks are also used to entertain audiences. Different classes of trucks are raced in competitions, and monster trucks, which are modified pickup trucks, appear in shows where they race through mud pits, in obstacle courses, and perform stunts.

Grocery store chains that deliver fresh foods to stores daily need to transport their products both long and short distances. Tractor-trailers are used to haul goods long distances, and smaller delivery trucks are often used for shorter distances.

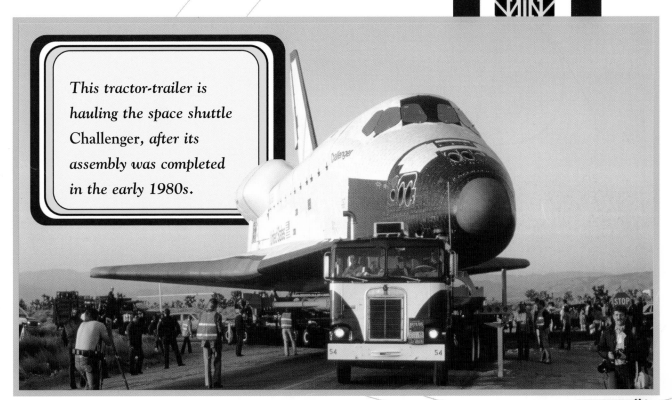

This tractor-trailer is hauling the space shuttle Challenger, *after its assembly was completed in the early 1980s.*

5

Early Trucks

Before trucks and other motor vehicles were invented, people used carriages or wagons pulled by horses to get from place to place. Early inventors attached steam engines to carriages, making motorized vehicles. Improved engines and new chassis designs led to the development of the truck.

The First Steam Wagon

In 1769, Nicolas-Joseph Cugnot, a member of the French army, built the first automobile powered by a steam engine. His vehicle was called *fardier à vapeur*, or steam wagon. It could travel at speeds of up to 2.5 miles per hour (four kilometers per hour) and pull 4.4 tons (four tonnes) of weight. Cugnot's steam wagon was used to carry cannon and other large weapons into battle. It had two wheels at the back and one in the front, which supported the steam boiler, or large tank where the steam was produced.

Steam Locomotive

English inventor Richard Trevithick also experimented with steam-powered vehicles. In 1802, Trevithick built the first steam locomotive, a railway vehicle that hauls train cars. Trevithick's locomotive hauled 70 passengers seated in five railroad cars, and ten tons (9.07 tonnes) of iron for more than nine miles (14.5 kilometers). The steam engine was improved, and beginning in the mid-1800s, inventors began to power carriages with steam engines for travel on roads, leading to the invention of cars and trucks.

Cugnot's steam wagon was steered with a tiller. A tiller is a horizontal bar the driver used to guide the wheel.

The First Trucks

Beginning in the late 1800s, motor vehicles were used to transport people from one place to another. Over time, people wanted larger vehicles that could also transport cargo. In 1895, German engineer Karl Benz built a truck powered by an internal combustion engine. Internal combustion engines burn a fuel, such as gasoline, rather than steam. German engineer Gottlieb Daimler designed and built his first truck in 1898. The engine was mounted on the back of the truck and was designed to run on gasoline, lamp fuel, and coal gas. Daimler's truck was fitted with thin wooden wheels covered with iron, which made them more **durable**. The chassis, or frame, of the truck had a suspension system made up of springs at the front and back, which allowed the vehicle to travel smoothly over the bumpy dirt roads of the day.

(above right) Before trucks were invented, heavy loads were carried on wagons pulled by horses.

This Daimler truck was built in 1904. Most early trucks looked like motorized wagons. Drivers sat in open areas at the front.

Going Commercial

In the early 1900s, vehicle manufactures began building trucks for commercial use, or for shipping goods from businesses to customers. Trucks were popular among business owners because of their speed and ability to carry large loads.

Building Routes

In the late 1800s and early 1900s, businesses in North America relied on the railroad and ships to transport their products over long distances. Roads at the time were still mostly dirt and did not run throughout the entire continent. As automobiles became more popular in the early 1900s, more roads were built and paved. By the mid-1900s, highways connected major cities, and trucks were delivering commercial products all over North America.

Winton Motor Company

The Winton Motor Carriage Company was one of the first American manufacturers to build commercial trucks. The company was established in 1897 by Scottish engineer Alexander Winton in Cleveland, Ohio. In 1898, Winton experimented with internal combustion engines and built his first truck, which was a delivery wagon. The engine had one **cylinder** and ran on gasoline. The truck was steered with a steering wheel rather than a tiller, which was common during this time. In 1900, Winton expanded his factory to include an area where only delivery wagons were built.

The first commercial uses for trucks were as delivery wagons that transported goods within communities.

The Industrial Age

Building trucks is also a commercial business. As the demand for trucks grew, automobile companies began looking for ways to speed up the manufacturing process. Henry Ford established the Ford Motor Company in 1903, in Dearborn, Michigan, and introduced the first moving assembly line in his factory in 1913. In an assembly line, vehicles traveled along conveyor belts to workers, who each installed a specific part. The assembly line reduced the amount of time and cost to build each vehicle, which lowered the purchase price. The Ford Motor Company built several types of trucks, including pickup trucks, which were built on the assembly line in 1925.

Advancements in Truck Design

Several advancements in truck design were made during and after World War II that made trucks more popular as commercial vehicles. Early trucks were fitted with solid rubber tires. Pneumatic tires, or tires that were filled with compressed air, were used on most trucks by the 1950s. Pneumatic tires made the ride smoother, which was an advantage when carrying cargo and passengers. Truck engines were also made more powerful, from having one or two cylinders in the early days to four, six, and eight cylinders. This gave trucks more power and allowed them to haul heavier loads. Engines that ran on **diesel** fuel also grew in popularity after World War II, especially in Europe. Diesel engines are more powerful and **fuel-efficient** than gas-powered engines, which makes them ideal for powering trucks.

This 1930 advertisement for Ford promoted their trucks' strength and dependability.

People realized the value of trucks during World War I. Trucks were used as ambulances and to transport supplies and soldiers.

Parts of a Truck

Truck designs differ depending on the jobs they are required to do, but all trucks have the same basic parts. These parts work together to help trucks do their jobs, and run safely and reliably.

Trailer

The trailer is the back section of a tractor-trailer that holds the cargo. The trailer is hauled by the tractor, or the front portion that consists of the cabin and engine.

Engine

Trucks are powered by internal combustion engines. Inside the engine, fuel is heated and mixed with air, which combusts, or explodes, within a cylinder. The combustion creates pressure that causes a piston, or thick disk, to move up and down within the cylinder. The piston pushes the fuel and air mixture through the cylinder to power the engine. The greater number of cylinders an engine has, the more power it produces.

Fifth wheel coupling

The trailer is connected to the tractor with a coupling called a fifth wheel coupling. The fifth wheel coupling is bolted onto the tractor's chassis, or frame. A coupling pin, which is attached to the trailer, fits inside the coupling, linking the two sections of a tractor-trailer together. The trailer is able to swivel around the coupling, which makes turning corners easier than if the truck was a large straight truck.

Transmission

The transmission is the system of gears and other parts that transmit, or send, power from the engine to the wheels. Different gears allow the wheels to turn at different speeds. Many tractor-trailers have manual transmissions, which means drivers change gears by hand using a **clutch** and gearshift. Some pickups, SUVs, and other trucks have automatic transmissions, which shift gears automatically depending on a truck's speed.

Suspension

The suspension is a system of springs, shock absorbers, and axles that support the weight of a truck. The suspension system contributes to the truck's **handling**, protects the truck from damage, and provides a more comfortable ride for drivers and passengers. The springs keep a truck from moving too much when the wheels move over rough roads or obstacles, such as speed bumps. The shocks keep a truck from bouncing when it drives over bumps.

Wheels

Wheels consist of tires fitted around metal frames. Each set of wheels turns on an axle, which is a long bar that also helps support a truck's weight. Tires are designed with different treads, or patterns, that affect how the tires grip different road surfaces.

Bed

Pickup trucks have beds, or open areas at the back where cargo is stored. Beds are available in different sizes, and most have walls to prevent loads from falling out. The most popular type of bed is the short bed, which is between six and 6.5 feet (1.8 and two meters) long. Short beds can carry large loads, but are not too long to make driving or parking the truck difficult.

The Cabin

The cabin, or cab, is the enclosed area where the driver and passengers sit. Features are added to cabs to make trucks more comfortable to drive, such as air conditioning, sound systems, and ergonomic seating, which lets drivers sit in a way that relieves pressure from their backs and **joints**.

Off-Road Trucks

An off-road truck is a vehicle that travels on paved roads as well as on rough terrain, such as over gravel, snow, and mud. Some people drive off-road trucks to enjoy the landscape of places that most vehicles cannot travel to, such as wilderness areas. Other drivers participate in off-road competitions, which include driving through mud pits, over sand dunes, and racing over rocks.

Off-Road Essentials

Off-road trucks are equipped with large tires that have deep treads, allowing them good **traction** with the ground. Traction is also achieved with four-wheel drive, or 4x4, which is a system that sends power from the engine to all four wheels. Most passenger vehicles have two-wheel drive, or power sent to only the two front wheels or two back wheels, which means they lose traction more easily in slippery or wet conditions than 4x4s. An off-road truck also has an increased ground clearance, which means that the bottom of the truck's frame is high above the ground. This allows off-road trucks to travel on uneven ground without objects, such as rocks, damaging the underside of the vehicle.

The suspension systems, or shock absorbers, springs, and axles, of off-road trucks must be strong enough to withstand the effects of driving through mud, and over dirt mounds, rocks, or other uneven surfaces.

Popular Off-Road Vehicles

Off-road vehicles were originally used by the military because they could travel over different types of terrain. Today, off-road vehicles, especially SUVs, are often purchased for their visual appeal and luxury features, such as **Global Positioning Systems**, or GPS, and are not used for off-road driving. Pickup trucks are popular off-road vehicles. Ford Motor Company's F-series trucks have been one of the best selling line of pickup trucks in the United States since the 1970s.

SUVs, such as this one built by Land Rover, are popular off-road vehicles. They are also powerful enough to tow boats and camping trailers.

Hummer of a Truck

The Hummer, manufactured by General Motors, is one of the largest SUVs on the market, and has been available to the public since 1995. An early version, called the M998 High Mobility Multipurpose Wheeled Vehicle, also known as the HMMWV or Humvee, was built for the United States armed forces in 1985. The Humvee was fitted with armor and weapons for patrolling war zones. Hummers share many of the same features as Humvees, including the frame, suspension, and transmission. A model designed as a pickup is also available, as well as a smaller, more fuel-efficient Hummer, called the H3.

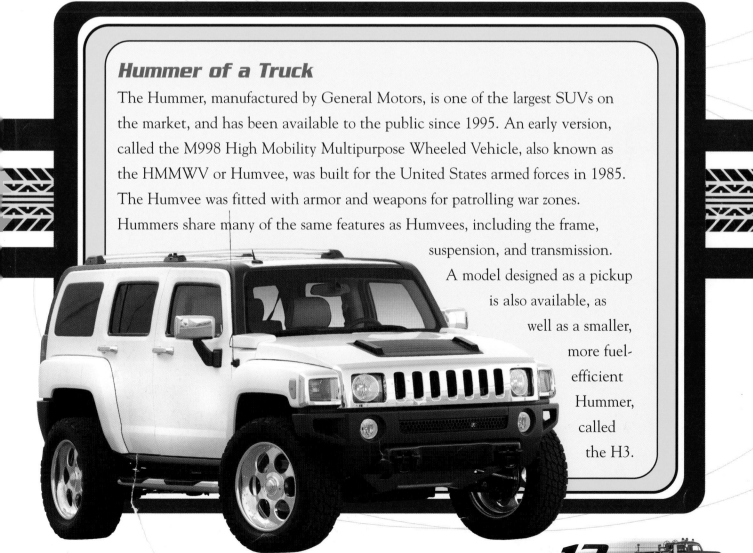

13

Off-Roading

Off-roading is a type of motorsport that involves racing off-road vehicles. There are many categories of off-roading, which feature different types of vehicles. One category is rock crawling, in which 4x4 vehicles drive over harsh terrain, such as mountain trails and foothills, and over rock piles. The event tests the skill of the driver and the vehicle rather than speed. The vehicles are equipped with larger than average tires and special suspension systems. Rock crawling competitions are usually comprised of an obstacle course 100 to 200 yards (91 to 183 meters)in length. Four-wheel drive vehicles are also used to compete in mud bogging competitions. In mud bogging, vehicles drive through areas of wet mud or clay as far as possible before getting stuck, and the winner is the driver who travels the furthest distance. The vehicles must have special mud tires to compete, which are wide and have large tread patterns.

This four-wheel drive pickup truck launches off a dirt mound during a race. The specialized suspension systems ensure the axles and other parts do not break when the truck lands. Some trucks also have roll cages, or strong frames built into the cab to protect drivers if the truck rolls onto its side or roof.

Parts of a Pickup Truck

Pickup trucks are often used as off-road vehicles, but are also purchased to "pick up" small loads or for towing. The open back of a pickup is called the bed, and is where loads are stored. The tailgate is the door at the back of the bed that flips down, making it easier to unload cargo. Some owners add box liners, which are large plastic boxes that fit into the bed to protect the paint job. Most cabs have one long seat, while others are extended cabs with four doors that feature two rows of seating.

Types of Pickups

There are different types of pickups available for people to buy. Compact pickups are the most common and are driven worldwide. They usually have six-cylinder engines, run on gasoline, and can tow up to 3,000 pounds (1,360 kilograms). Full-size pickup trucks are larger than compact trucks and are designed to carry and haul heavier loads. Most full-size pickups have eight- or ten-cylinder diesel engines.

(above) Many European manufacturers build coupe utility pickups, or "utes," which were originally developed in Australia. The cab of an ute looks like a car, but it has a bed at the back.

Full-size pickup trucks have the power to haul large trailers and campers.

The Big Ones

Tractor-trailers are powerful articulated trucks, also referred to as big rigs. They are designed to haul heavy loads long distances, and are important to companies that deliver products across countries or continents.

What is a Big Rig?

Big rigs are made up of two separate parts; the tractor is the front section that contains a large diesel engine and the cabin, and the trailer is the wheeled section at the back that is pulled by the tractor. In North America, tractor-trailers are commonly called eighteen-wheelers, because they are fitted with 18 wheels to support the heavy weight of the loads they carry. The tractors usually have three axles. The front axle is called the steer axle, and supports two wheels, one at each end of the axle. There are two axles at the back of the tractor, called the drive axles, and each is equipped with four wheels. The trailer usually has two axles supporting the back end, each with four wheels. In the United States, the maximum load weight for an eighteen-wheeler is between 80,000 and 99,000 pounds (36,287 and 44,906 kilograms).

(above) The dials and switches on a big rig's dashboard lets the driver monitor and control the truck's systems.

(right) Most big rigs have hoods that flip forward so mechanics can get to the engines.

Road Trains

Road trains are big rigs made of tractors that pull more than one trailer. They have powerful engines and are used to transport large heavy loads, including livestock, and building materials, such as gravel. They are driven in **remote** areas of Canada, the United States, and Australia. Australia is home to the largest road trains in the world. They were developed to transport food, fuel, and other products to communities in remote areas. It is common for Australian road trains to have up to six trailers attached to a single tractor, with each trailer holding up to 140 tons (127 tonnes) of freight. Road trains are difficult to maneuver due to their size, so it is safest for the vehicles to travel on roads that are clear of traffic. When the vehicles near populated areas, the multiple trailers are detached and then fastened to other individual tractors.

Tractor-trailers stop at weigh stations to ensure the loads they carry are within safety limits.

Road trains are commonly used to transport goods in the Australian outback. In 2006, a road train in Queensland, Australia, had 104 trailers and measured 4,837 feet (1,474 meters) long!

The Trucking Life

Truck drivers are responsible for hauling cargo short or long distances. Long hauls can take drivers away from their homes for days or even weeks. Drivers must be careful to avoid accidents to ensure their own safety as well as the safety of the cargo and other drivers on the road.

Licenses and Training

Drivers must have special driving licenses to operate commercial trucks. In the United States, there are different classes of Commercial Driver's Licenses (CDL), including ones for tankers and tractor-trailers. Training is also required. For example, drivers that haul dangerous goods, such as **flammable** chemicals, must undergo special training to learn how to deal with emergency situations, such as if their load catches fire.

Trucking Safety

Each country has laws that limit the number of hours a truck driver is able to drive. This is done to prevent truck drivers from becoming tired and causing accidents. In the United States, truck drivers are allowed to drive for 11 hours, at which time they must take a ten-hour break. A device called a tachometer is fitted to the truck to monitor the speed the truck is traveling at and the number of hours the truck has been driven.

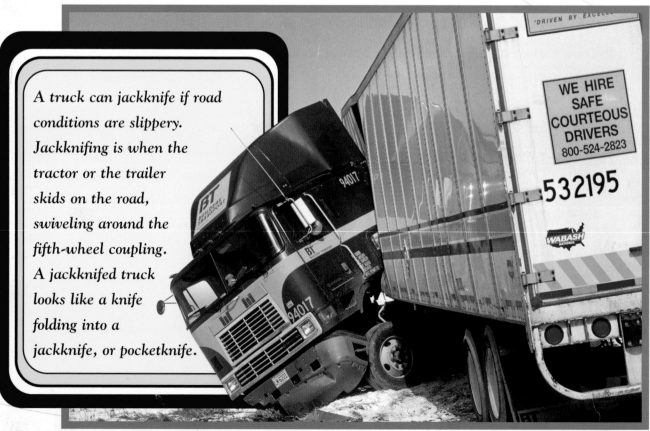

A truck can jackknife if road conditions are slippery. Jackknifing is when the tractor or the trailer skids on the road, swiveling around the fifth-wheel coupling. A jackknifed truck looks like a knife folding into a jackknife, or pocketknife.

WE HIRE SAFE COURTEOUS DRIVERS
800-524-2823

532195

A Home Away from Home

Some truck drivers travel long distances and are away from home for weeks at a time. Their trucks have sleepers, or compartments, attached to the cab that are equipped with a bed, television, radio, and other features for the driver's comfort. Truck drivers also stop at truck stops, which are located on or near major roads, to rest and refresh themselves before continuing their routes. Truck stops consist of fueling stations, convenience stores, restaurants, and often have showers, TVs, and internet access the drivers can use.

This truck stop has an eye-catching sign.

Staying in Touch

Citizens' Band radio, or CB, is a radio system that allows people to communicate on a selection of radio channels. CB was established in the United States in 1945, and is still used today by some businesses. Communication is possible within a range of one to five miles (1.6 to eight kilometers). Truck drivers use Citizens' Band radio to communicate with their employers and with emergency services in the event of an accident. Many trucks are also equipped with satellite radio systems, which transmit signals from **satellites**, rather than **transmission towers** as other radio systems do. Satellite radio signals can be heard clearly from much farther away than CB radio signals.

Trucks to the Rescue

Before trucks were invented, people used horse-drawn carriages, bicycles, and traveled on foot to respond to emergencies, which meant response times were slow. Today, trucks, including fire trucks and ambulances, are used to reach emergencies quickly.

Fire Trucks

Fire trucks are large trucks that transport firefighters, rescue tools, and equipment to fires. A pumper is a fire truck that has a tank that holds about 1,000 gallons (3,785 liters) of water and many fire hoses. Ladder trucks are equipped with ladders that extend more than 110 feet (30 meters) into the air. Firefighters climb the ladders to spray water directly onto fires, and rescue people from burning buildings.

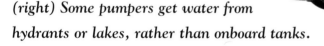

(right) Some pumpers get water from hydrants or lakes, rather than onboard tanks.

Ambulances

Ambulances are used to transport people to hospitals quickly. They carry emergency medical personnel and equipment to car accidents and other emergencies. Most ambulances are built on the same chassis, or frames, as vans. Ambulances are equipped with sirens and flashing lights to warn drivers and pedestrians of their approach.

(left) Ambulances have GPSs, so drivers find the fastest routes to emergencies.

Tow Trucks

Tow trucks are used to remove vehicles that are broken down or damaged in accidents from the road. They are also used to retrieve vehicles that are stuck in snow, mud, or rivers, and are used to **impound** vehicles that are illegally parked on public and private properties. Tow trucks have powerful engines and can haul vehicles weighing up to 50 tons (45 tonnes). Some tow trucks have beds at the back that are lowered to the ground, while others use a **winch**, or crane, to lift and haul vehicles.

Some tow trucks raise only the front wheels of a vehicle, as long as the vehicle is not too damaged, and tow it behind the truck

Armored Trucks

Armored trucks are used to protect passengers or items inside from harm. Military trucks, which are trucks used by a country's armed forces, are heavily armored with metal plates for protection against bullets, bombs, missiles, and **shrapnel**. Weapons, such as machine guns, are also added to military trucks that enter combat situations. Many passenger vehicles are armored to protect people, including politicians and religious leaders, who are often targets of violence.

Armored trucks are used to transport valuables and money to banks and other locations. Guards are onboard to prevent hijackings.

On the Building Site

The success of a construction project relies on planning, which includes ensuring the proper trucks and machines are used. Trucks are used to help construct buildings, and haul materials, such as cement, dirt, and gravel, to and away from job sites.

Dump Trucks

A dump truck has an open bin on the back used to carry materials such as gravel, rock, and dirt. These trucks move loads from one location to another. Once the dump truck reaches its destination, the bin is raised and dumps the load behind the truck. There are many different types of dump trucks. A standard dump truck is made up of a tractor with the open bin attached to it. Standard dump trucks have one axle at the front, and one or two axles at the rear that have dual, or two, wheels on each end. Off-road dump trucks are used on construction sites to haul very heavy loads. These are often much larger than standard or articulated trucks and have big wheels that allow them to be used off-road, or over rough terrain.

Articulated dump trucks are made up of a tractor and an open bin that are hinged together, but unlike articulated tractor-trailers, the bin cannot be separated from the tractor.

Concrete Mixers

A concrete mixer is a truck used to transport concrete to job sites. Concrete is a strong material used to make building foundations and sidewalks. A concrete mixer has a large rotating tank, or drum, on the back that churns a mixture of sand, gravel, powdered cement, and water. When this mixture is left to settle, it hardens into concrete. The tank continuously turns to keep the mixture from hardening before it is delivered to the job site. When it is ready to be used, the concrete is poured from the tank onto chutes or through pipes.

Mobile Cranes

Mobile cranes are hoisting, or lifting, machines mounted onto trucks. Cranes hoist and move heavy objects using cables attached to arms called telescopic booms. A hook is suspended from the top of the crane, and is used to move objects. Mobile cranes are commonly used on construction sites to lift heavy materials, such as steel beams. The crane sits on top of an outrigger, which is a frame projecting from the truck that keeps the crane stabilized. Most mobile cranes can lift objects weighing from ten to 100 tons (nine to 91 tonnes). An operator sits in the crane's cabin, using levers and switches to direct the crane's movements.

(above) Mixers have tanks that hold about 40,000 pounds (18,144 kilograms) of concrete.

(below) Mounting a crane to a truck allows it to be moved from site to site.

Working Hard

Trucks play an important role in helping people complete work. Before trucks and other machinery were invented, people had to rely on manual labor to complete many tasks. Today, many trucks are specially designed to help complete specific jobs.

Garbage Trucks

Garbage trucks are designed to store trash and transport it to landfills. Rear loaders are garbage trucks that service residential areas. Workers empty garbage cans and throw garbage bags into an opening at the back of the truck. Businesses that produce a lot of waste are serviced by front loader trucks. Front loaders have forks at the front of the trucks that grip dumpsters and other waste containers, lift them over the truck, and flip them upside down to empty their contents into a bin at the back of the truck. After the waste is dumped, a compactor called a packer blade compresses, or flattens, the waste and pushes it to the rear of the truck.

Trucks are used to collect recyclable materials, such as newspapers, cans, and glass, and transport them to recycling facilities where they are made into new materials. Recyclables are sorted into categories, such as plastic, aluminum, and paper by the workers that collect them.

Rear loaders also have compactors that compress waste.

Tankers

Tankers are trucks used to transport liquids, such as gasoline, or powders, such as powdered milk, in bulk, or large quantities. The trucks have cylindrical tanks. Some tanks are designed to hold only one load, and others are made up of different compartments, each holding a different product. The tanks are specially designed for different uses. For example, some tanks are refrigerated for carrying food products that must be kept at specific temperatures. Septic trucks are also tankers. They drain septic waste, or sewage, from tanks in neighborhoods, and then dispose of the waste at collection sites.

(above right) Large tankers hold up to 9,000 gallons (34,069 liters), while small tankers, which carry loads within communities, carry less than 3,000 gallons (11,356 liters).

Logging Trucks

A logging truck is a flatbed trailer, which is a type of tractor-trailer with no sides or top. The logging industry cuts down trees to supply raw materials to industries that use wood products, such as sawmills where logs are sawed into boards, and the paper industry that uses wood pulp to make paper and other products. The logs on a flatbed trailer are secured by strong chains or cables. Some logging trucks are powerful enough to haul more than three trailers, each carrying 50 tons (45 tonnes) of wood.

Logging trucks that drive on public roads have to conform to regulations that specify how much weight they can carry and how long each trailer can be.

25

Truck Racing

Trucks are not only used for hauling, but are driven for recreational purposes as well. Truck racing is a motor sport in which trucks are raced on circuits, or tracks. Today, truck racing is gaining popularity in Europe and North America.

The Pickup Series is a set of races that take place in the United Kingdom for pickup trucks.

European Truck Racing

Grand Prix Truck Racing is a popular racing series in Europe that features trucks similar to the tractors of a big rig that have been modified to reach high speeds. Today, the series is made up of 30 teams from countries around Europe, and the races are enjoyed by thousands of fans. A motor sport organization called the Federation Internationale de l'Automobile (F.I.A.) establishes the technical regulations, such as the design and safety standards trucks must comply with, and the rules drivers must obey. For safety reasons trucks are not allowed to exceed 100 miles per hour (160 kilometers per hour).

Grand Prix Races

Grand Prix truck races take place on circuits of different shapes, each posing challenges for the truck and the driver. A race is usually made up of eight to 12 laps. Racing trucks are road-driven trucks that have been modified into racing machines, and must weigh more than 12,125 pounds (5,500 kilograms). The trucks are powered by diesel engines, and superchargers are added. A supercharger is a mechanical device that forces more air and fuel into the engine to increase its power. The trucks are also fitted with racing tires, for increased traction.

NASCAR Craftsman Series

The Craftsman Truck Series is a popular racing series that features modified pickup trucks. The series is one of three divisions of the National Association for Stock Car Automobile Racing (NASCAR), the largest official body of motor sports in the United States. In 1993, a group of racers built a prototype of a racing pickup truck, which was raced in demonstrations during the Daytona 500 race in 1994. Soon, racing pickups grew in popularity, and NASCAR created the SuperTruck series in 1995. The name of the series was changed to the Craftsman Truck Series the following year. During the first year of the series, the truck races were held on short circuits that covered no more than 125 miles (200 kilometers), and featured about 150 laps. Today, the trucks race 200 to 250 laps of longer circuits that cover about 250 miles (400 kilometers).

Each driver who races in the Craftsman truck series must wear a helmet, and fire-resistant coveralls, gloves, and boots for protection in case the engine ignites during a crash.

Climbing the Peak

The Pikes Peak International Hill Climb, also called "The Race to the Clouds," is an annual uphill race to the summit, or peak, of Pikes Peak, a mountain in Colorado, United States. Different classes of motorcycles and automobiles, including trucks, have competed in the race since 1916. The course is 12.4 miles (20 kilometers) long, and is made up of more than 156 turns. Drivers race their trucks to the summit, which is at an elevation of 14,110 feet (4,300 kilometers).

Monster Trucks

Monster trucks are large trucks that have huge customized wheels and powerful engines. Millions of monster truck fans cram stadiums and arenas every year to watch their favorite monster trucks crush old cars, perform stunts, and get sprayed with mud as they race through obstacle courses.

The First Monster Truck

In 1974, Bob Chandler, from Missouri, in the United States, bought a blue 4x4 Ford F-250 pickup truck. At his car repair shop, Chandler customized his truck by adding features such as large tires. To make steering his heavy truck easier, Chandler invented four-wheel steering, which is a system that allows a driver to turn both the front wheels and back wheels. Chandler called his truck Bigfoot. Bigfoot is considered the world's first monster truck.

Parts of a Monster Truck

Monster trucks usually weigh about 9,900 pounds (4,500 kilograms), and are almost ten feet (three meters) high. The trucks' bodies are made of **fiberglass**, which is easier to repair than metal and is also lighter, allowing the trucks to go faster. Most monster trucks have engines from other pickup trucks or from fast cars such as Ford Mustangs and Chevrolet Corvettes. They have large terra tires, which are about 5.5 feet (1.7 meters) high. Terra tires are designed for farm machinery, and are ideal for driving in mud.

In 1982, Chandler impressed audiences at a motor show by driving over old junk cars and crushing them with his Bigfoot truck. Today, Bigfoot trucks perform all over the world.

Monster Competitions

The popularity of monster trucks grew in the 1980s. The first monster truck competition was held in 1984, and included Bigfoot, and other trucks, such as Barefoot and King Kong. By the mid-1980s, monster trucks were also mud bogging, or racing through deep mud pits. Obstacle courses and freestyle were added later. In freestyle, drivers perform stunts with their trucks, such as spinning in circles at high speeds.

Monster Truck Safety

In 1988, Bob Chandler formed the Monster Truck Racing Association (MTRA), which is an organization that created the performance and safety rules for monster truck events. Officials inspect each monster truck before events to ensure they have the required safety equipment. Drivers are securely strapped with a harness inside roll cages, which are strong frames that are built around the cabs. Roll cages protect the driver from injury if the monster truck rolls over. Each monster truck has a kill switch, which turns off the engine if the truck rolls over or the driver loses control. All monster truck drivers are required to wear helmets, and fire-resistant clothing for protection in case a truck is in an accident and catches fire. Emergency medical technicians, or EMTs, are at every monster truck event to deal with emergencies.

Monster trucks can jump distances of up to 95 feet (38 meters), and can be launched up to 15 feet (eight meters) in to the air.

29

Super Cool Trucks

Many trucks are customized to make them look cool and drive differently than other vehicles, while other trucks are customized to the extreme.

Lowriders

A lowrider is a car or truck that has been lowered so that it drives close to the ground. This is done by altering a vehicle's suspension systems, many of which are **hydraulically-powered**. Drivers use hydraulic suspensions to make one end of their vehicle bounce off the ground as high as six feet (1.8 meters). Lowriders were developed in Los Angeles, California, during the late 1930s. They were created by modifying inexpensive cars, such as models manufactured by Ford and Chevrolet. Today, many lowriders are equipped with stylish accessories, such as custom upholstery, steering wheels, and hubcaps, as well as chrome- or gold-spoked wheels, and are considered "cool rides."

Shockwave Jet Truck

Shockwave is a 6,800-pound (3,048-kilogram) truck powered by three jet engines that shoot flames from the exhaust pipes. Shockwave can reach speeds of up to 376 miles per hour (605 kilometers per hour). The truck is displayed in motor shows, where it amazes audiences by racing an airplane that flies overhead. When the race is over, a parachute is released from the back of the truck to help slow Shockwave down.

(above) Lowriders are often made cool by giving them custom paint jobs.

Shockwave accelerates from zero to 300 miles per hour (483 kilometers per hour) in just 11 seconds.

Robosaurus

In 1990, a monster truck called Robosaurus began appearing at motor sport events. Robosaurus is a giant robot modeled after a Tyrannosaurus rex, and is controlled by a driver that sits inside its head. It weighs 12,270 pounds (5,660 kilograms) and is more than 40 feet (12 meters) tall when fully extended. Robosaurus picks up cars and even small airplanes with its claws and tears them apart with its steel teeth. It even breathes 25-foot (seven-meter) flames from its mouth! When Robosaurus is not performing, it transforms into a trailer that is hauled throughout the United States.

Glossary

clutch A device that engages and disengages a vehicle's gears

commercial Relating to business

couplings A device that connects two things

customized Made to suit a person's taste

cylinder An engine chamber where combustion takes place

diesel A type of fuel often made from petroleum

durable Long lasting

fiberglass A material made from fibers of glass

flammable Able to catch fire easily

fuel-efficient Burning less fuel than other engines while creating the same amount of power

Global Positioning Systems Computerized systems that provide directions to drivers

handling The way a truck takes corners and reacts to going over bumpy roads

hijackings Stopping a vehicle to rob it, or take it over

hydraulically Done using a machine that has parts that move due to pressure caused by a moving liquid

impound To seize, or take

industries Businesses that make and sell products

joints Parts on the body that bend, such as elbows and knees

remote Far away from large populations of people

response time The time it takes to get to a place

satellite An object orbiting the Earth that sends and receives communication signals

shrapnel The fragments of a bomb

steam engine An engine powered by steam, which was created by burning wood or coal

traction Ability to grip a surface

transmission towers Towers that send and relay radio and television signals

whitewall tires Tires that have a band of white rubber on their sidewalls

winch A device that hauls objects using a cable that is wound around a drum, or cylinder

World War I A conflict that took place from 1914 to 1918 and involved many countries

Index

Printed in the U.S.A.